MW01130044

THERE'S GOLD IN CALI!

WHAT HAPPENED DURING THE GOLD RUSH?

US History Books for Kids

Children's American History

BABY PROFESSOR

EDUCATION KIDS

Speedy Publishing LLC

40 E. Main St. #1156

Newark, DE 19711

www.speedypublishing.com

Copyright 2017

All Rights reserved. No part of this book may be reproduced or used in any way or form or by any means whether electronic or mechanical, this means that you cannot record or photocopy any material ideas or tips that are provided in this book.

The California Gold Rush occurred between the years of 1848 and 1855, at which time gold had been discovered at Sutter's Mill. More than 300,000 people headed to California to dig for gold so they could strike it rich! In this book, we will be learning about how it was discovered and how it affected California, as well as countries around the world.

DISCOVERING GOLD IN CALIFORNIA

Gold was originally discovered at Sutter's Mill by James Marshall, near the town of Coloma, California. He found some shiny flakes of gold along the river while he was constructing a sawmill for John Sutter. He let John known about his discovery and they attempted to keep their find a secret. Word soon got out, however, and prospectors rushed to California to find their own gold.

Sutter's Mill

Gold Washing in California

WHO WERE THE FORTY-NINERS?

Prior to the gold rush, there were about only 14,000 non-Native Americans that lived in California. This changed quickly and in 1848 about 6,000 people arrived, followed by about 90,000 in 1849, in their hunt for gold. They arrived from all parts of the world and became known as the 49ers. Some were from the America, but others came from places such as Mexico, China, Australia, and Europe.

WOMEN DURING THE GOLD RUSH

There were also a small number of women in the Gold Rush. Only 700 of the 40,000 people that arrived in the San Francisco Harbor by ship in 1849 were women. The roles of the women varied included prostitution, married, single entrepreneurs, wealthy, and poor.

California Gold Rush - Chinese Miners

The various ethnicities of the women included African-American, Anglo-American, Native, Hispanic, European, Jewish, and Chinese. They came for various reasons: some refused to be left behind and came along with their husbands; some came after their husband sent for them; and some (widows and singles) came for the economic opportunities and the adventure.

Some people died along the trail from accidents, fever, cholera, and many other reasons, often causing women to become widows before ever arriving in California. Once they arrived in California, frequently women would become widows because of mining accidents, diseases, or mining disputes between the husbands. Living in the goldfields provided women with opportunities to break away from their conventional way of life.

DIGGING FOR GOLD

Many of the prospectors that arrived first made a bunch of money and would often make ten times in one day what they would make at a typical job. The original miners panned for gold. More complex methods were later developed which allowed several miners to work with each other and search bigger amounts of gravel.

PANNING FOR GOLD

One of the methods that the miners used for separating the gold from the gravel and dirt was referred to as panning. As they panned for gold, the miners would put water and gravel in a pan and then shake it back and forth. Since gold is heavy, eventually, it would work its way towards the bottom of the pan.

Panning for Gold

Gold Sand in a Pan

Once the miner had shaken the pan for a while, the gold would be found on the bottom of the pan and the gravel and dirt would be towards the top. The miner can then remove the gold, set it aside, and return to pan for additional gold.

WHERE DID IT GO?

Once the gold was extracted, it took several paths. Most of the gold was first used locally for purchasing supplies, food, and for the miners' lodging. It would also go towards entertainment, including gambling, alcohol, and prostitutes as well as to enjoy a traveling theater. They would use their recently discovered gold for these transactions, which would be weighed out carefully. In turn, these vendors and merchants would use the gold for purchasing supplies from ship captains or packers that brought their goods to California.

The Town of Dry Diggings, California

Gold Mining in California

The gold would then leave California aboard mules or ships to deliver to the makers of goods throughout the world. Another path would be the miners, after obtaining a sufficient amount of gold, would send it home, or return home with their "diggings". One example is an estimate of about $80 million worth of the California gold sent by French merchants and prospectors, to their homeland of France.

With progression of the Gold Rush, gold dealers and local banks started issuing "drafts" or "banknotes", a form of paper currency accepted by the locals, in exchange for their gold, and private cold coins were created by private mints. In 1854, with the start of the San Francisco Mint, gold bullion would be made into gold coins to be circulated. Later, gold was sent to U.S. national banks from California banks and exchanged for national paper currency that could be utilized for California's booming economy.

San Francisco Mint Building

Gold Prospecting Tools

WHAT SUPPLIES DID THE MINERS REQUIRE?

These thousands of miners all required supplies. The supplies they needed typically would include a shovel, a mining pan, as well as a pick for mining. In addition, they would also need food and living supplies including bacon, coffee, beans, sugar, flour, a tent, bedding, a kettle, and a lamp.

The business and store owners who sold these supplies to the miners had often become wealthier than the miners. These business owners could sell the necessary items to the miners at very high prices, which the miners were more than willing to pay.

Miners With Gold in a Pan

BOOMTOWNS

As gold would be discovered in a new area, the miners would move to the new location and start a mining camp. These camps would sometimes grow rapidly into towns known as boomtowns. The cities of Columbia and San Francisco are two examples of boomtowns that started during the gold rush.

ECONOMIC STIMULATION THROUGHOUT THE WORLD

Economies throughout the world were also stimulated by the Gold Rush. Farmers in Hawaii, Australia, and Chile discovered a new market for their food; goods manufactured by the British were now in high demand; prefabricated houses and clothing arrived from China.

Gold Rush

Edward Hargraves

The large amounts of California gold that was returned to these countries to pay for the goods proceeded to raise prices as well as created jobs throughout the world. Edward Hargraves, an Australian prospector, noted the similarities between the geography of his home country and California, and returned home to discover gold and sparked what became known as the Australian gold rushes.

In 1863, following the end of the Gold Rush, a groundbreaking ceremony was held in Sacramento for the western portion of the First Transcontinental Railroad. About six years later the line was completed, financed with some of the money gained from the Gold Rush, and linked California to the central and eastern portion of the United States. Travel could now be completed in days that previously would take weeks or months.

First Transcontinental Railroad

Bodie, Ghost Town

GHOST TOWNS

Eventually, most of the boomtowns were abandoned and became ghost towns. Once an area ran out of gold, the miners would move on to find the next location for panning gold. The businesses would shut down and the town would become empty and abandoned. Bodie, California is one such example of a ghost town, and is now a popular attraction for tourists.

CHARACTERISTICS AND PROPERTIES OF GOLD

Gold appears as a shiny yellow metal under typical conditions. It is very heavy and dense, but it is also somewhat soft.

In addition to being a beautiful metal, it is also an excellent conductor of heat and electricity. Gold is also one of the metals that is most resistant to rust and corrosion when exposed to water and air.

WHERE CAN GOLD BE FOUND ON EARTH?

Gold is a very rare element. Since it does not react with too many other elements, Gold is often found in the Earth's crust in its native form, or mixed with various other metals, such as silver. It can be found in tiny fragments in sandy riverbeds or in underground veins.

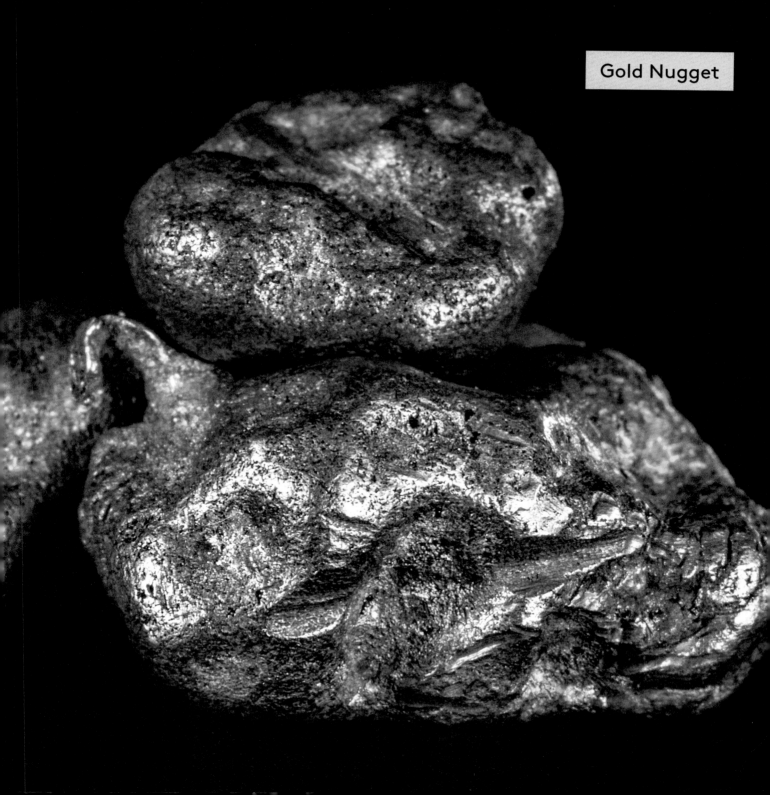
Gold Nugget

It can be found in ocean water as well. The process for retrieving it from the ocean water, however, costs more than the value of the gold.

HOW IS GOLD USED TODAY?

It has been used to make coins and jewelry for thousands of years and continues to be used today for jewelry as well as some coins that are collector's editions. Gold is also known to be a reliable and important investment.

Gold Coins

Gold Ring

When it is used for coins for as jewelry, it typically is not pure gold. Pure gold is known as 24 karat gold and is quite soft. It is generally mixed with additional metals like silver or copper to make it harder and durable.

Gold is also useful in the electronics industry since it is a good conductor of electricity and it is resistant to corrosion. Electrical connectors and contacts have a gold plating for reliability and protection.

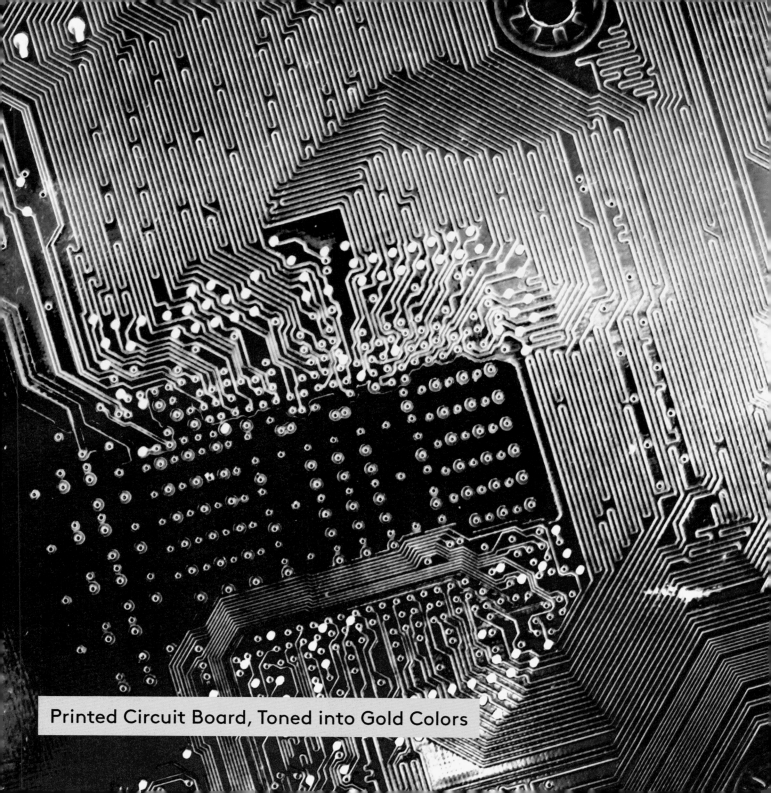

Printed Circuit Board, Toned into Gold Colors

Gold Nuggets

Some of the other uses for gold include cancer treatment, dental work, heat shielding, as well as decorative uses including gold plating and gold threading.

HOW WAS GOLD DISCOVERED?

Gold has been around since ancient times. Ancient Egypt used gold more than 5000 years ago. It has since them been known as a substance of wealth and value.

The Gold Rush was a great experience for most of the people involved. San Francisco had a population of about 1,000 when the gold was first discovered and only a few years later had more than 30,000 residents.

Other gold rushes in the United States include the Alaskan Klondike gold rush and the Pike's Peak gold rush that occurred in Colorado. For additional about these gold rushes, you can visit your local library, research the internet, and ask questions of your teachers, family, and friends.

Carthage
Cumberland
13
40
49
210
Macon
Columbus
Oglethorpe

Visit

BABY PROFESSOR
EDUCATION KIDS

www.BabyProfessorBooks.com

to download Free Baby Professor eBooks
and view our catalog of new and exciting
Children's Books

73202612R00038

Made in the USA
San Bernardino, CA
02 April 2018